D1247292

ZOO ANIMALS
IN THE WILD

GIANT PANDA

JINNY JOHNSON
ILLUSTRATED BY GRAHAM ROSEWARNE

A⁺
Smart Apple Media

Published by Smart Apple Media

2140 Howard Drive West, North Mankato, Minnesota 56003

Designed by Helen James

Illustrated by Graham Rosewarne

Photographs by China Span (Keren Su), Corbis (Bettmann, Tom Brakefield,
Tim Davis, PARKER HANK/CORBIS SYGMA, Reuters, Keren Su,
VAUGHN BILL/CORBIS SYGMA)

Printed and bound in Thailand

Library of Congress Cataloging-in-Publication Data

Johnson, Jinny.
Giant panda / by Jinny Johnson.
p. cm. — (Zoo animals in the wild)
Includes index.
ISBN 1-58340-645-X
1. Giant panda—Juvenile literature. I. Title.

QL737.C214J634 2005
599.789—dc22   2004065341

First Edition

9 8 7 6 5 4 3 2 1

Contents

Giant pandas

With its big, round head, black eye patches, and fluffy ears, the giant panda is one of the most recognizable animals in the world.

Although it may look cute and cuddly, the giant panda is a kind of bear. Like most bears, it is a large animal that weighs more than most full-grown people. A panda's body is

A panda's black and white fur is very thick and woolly.

There are about 100 giant pandas living in zoos in China, Europe, the United States, and Japan. Zoo pandas are all born in zoos. They aren't taken from the wild.

chunky and rounded, and it has a short tail. Most of the panda's fur is white, but it has black markings on its face, legs, and shoulders. It has big, strong teeth and powerful claws.

All pandas have black ears and black eye rings. But each animal has slightly different markings around its mouth.

At home in the wild

Wild giant pandas live in forests high in the mountains of China, where it is cool, misty, and often wet. A panda doesn't have a regular den but sometimes finds shelter in a hollow tree or cave.

In the winter, it snows in the mountains where pandas live, and it gets very cold.

A panda grows thick fur in the winter to keep warm, then loses some fur in the summer.

Pandas don't mind, though, because their furry coat keeps them warm. The fur has an oily surface that makes water run off of it. This keeps the panda dry.

No one knows what purpose the black and white markings on the panda's fur serve. Some people think that they might help pandas find each other in the forests when it's time to mate.

Evergreen trees and bamboo plants grow in the panda's mountain home.

At home in the zoo

Giant pandas are some of the most popular of all zoo animals. Zoo pandas need an outdoor area with rocks and trees where they can climb and exercise. Their zoo home must also have an indoor shelter where they can rest, sleep, and get away from zoo visitors when they want to.

Some of the newest panda enclosures have special rocky areas that are kept cool and damp—just like the pandas' home in the wild. Pandas also like to have a pool of water to splash in. When they come out, they shake themselves dry.

Snow in the zoo makes it feel like home!

These pandas are having fun on the climbing frame at the National Zoo in Washington, D.C.

On the move

Pandas move on all fours most of the time. They usually walk slowly and quietly, but they can move faster and even gallop a short distance. Pandas can also stand up on their back legs for a short time if they need to reach something.

Most pandas are good tree climbers. They come down backwards, arm over arm, just like people do. Each panda moves around its own territory but doesn't travel very far. A panda usually walks only about

A tree is a comfortable place to sit and rest for a while.

Since pandas don't travel very far in the wild, they don't need a very big home to roam around in the zoo.

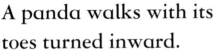
A panda walks with its toes turned inward.

1,800 feet (550 m) a day—about as far as four or five city blocks. The territories of several pandas may overlap, so the animals may come across each other once in a while, but they don't spend much time together.

A panda can stand—but not walk—on its hind legs.

A panda's day

Finding food and eating take up most of a panda's day. Pandas may be active at any time of the day or night, but they are usually busiest around dawn and in the early evening. At least once a day, a panda needs to find some water to drink.

Pandas spend up to 10 hours a day sleeping or resting. A panda doesn't make a bed for itself. Instead, it just lies down under the nearest tree, often going back to its favorite spots.

A panda laps up fresh water with its tongue.

A panda sleeps lying on its back or curled up on its side. It sometimes uses its back leg as a pillow or holds one paw over its eyes.

Pandas don't need to spend much time keeping themselves clean. They just roll in dirt or sand to get rid of any insects that may be in their fur.

Pandas usually sleep two to four hours at a time.

A panda enclosure often includes a sandpit in which the panda can roll to clean its fur.

Panda food

Pandas feed on a plant called bamboo. Bamboo is a kind of grass that grows in the forests where pandas live. There aren't many nutrients in bamboo, so the panda has to eat a lot of it—about 28 pounds (12.5 kg) a day. That's the same as eating about 25 large heads of lettuce!

An adult panda's 42 teeth are wide and strong.

A panda carefully chooses which pieces of bamboo to eat.

Bamboo is a tough plant, but the panda has big, broad teeth and strong jaws for crushing and chewing its food.

Pandas don't eat many other kinds of food, but they will sometimes nibble a few other plants or even catch a small animal such as a mouse.

How a panda eats

A giant panda has a special sixth finger, like a thumb, on each front paw. It can grip bamboo stems between this thumb and its first finger—just like people hold things. Other bears cannot do this.

The panda sits down on the ground to eat so that its front paws are free to handle the bamboo.

Pandas spend about 12 hours a day eating.

16

The panda's extra "thumb" gives it a strong grip.

The panda strips away the tough, outer layer of the bamboo stem with its teeth to get at the softer parts inside. It also picks off the leaves with its fingers and puts them into its mouth.

Zoo pandas eat bamboo, too. They're also given small amounts of other treats such as sugarcane, carrots, apples, and sweet potatoes.

Keeping in touch

Wild pandas spend most of their time by themselves, except when they're looking after their young. Pandas are quiet animals, but they do make some sounds.

When pandas meet, they may make a bleating call—a little like a sheep or goat. To scare off an enemy, such as a wild dog, a panda may bark or make a chomping sound, bringing its teeth together. A baby panda squeals loudly if it's frightened or gets separated from its mother.

A panda scratches a tree trunk as a message to other pandas.

Zoos used to keep pandas by themselves. Now zoos are finding that young pandas can live happily together and enjoy each other's company.

Pandas also keep in touch by smell. As they wander around the forest, they scratch trees to tell other pandas that they've been there. They may also leave scent messages on trees by spraying a thick liquid from a gland near their tail.

A panda may stand on its front paws to leave a scent mark on a tree.

Panda babies

A giant panda gives birth to her cub in a shelter such as a cave or hollow tree. Pandas usually have one baby at a time, but sometimes twins are born.

The newborn panda is tiny—about the size of a small rat. It is blind and helpless, with a scattering of white fur on its little, pink body. The mother looks after her baby by herself. She doesn't leave it at all for the first two weeks, even to eat or drink. She sits cradling her baby

If a mother panda needs to move her baby, she picks it up very gently in her mouth.

in her arms while it feeds on her milk. After each feeding, the mother licks her baby to keep it clean.

A mother panda is at least 900 times heavier than her newborn baby.

When a zoo panda gives birth to twins, the keepers help her take care of the babies. Every day, they switch the babies so that each one has a day with its mother, then a day with the keepers. The keepers bottle-feed the baby pandas.

Growing up

By the time it's a month old, the panda cub is beginning to grow its black and white fur. Its eyes open a few weeks later. The baby grows quickly.

By the time it's three or four months old, it weighs about 13 pounds (5.8 kg)—nearly 60 times as much as it did when it was born.

A panda's milk is rich and fatty, so her cub grows fast.

A panda cub feeds on its mother's milk until it is about nine months old, but it starts to eat some bamboo, too, when it's five or six months old. The baby must stay close to its mother. If it strays too far, it could be attacked by wild dogs, weasels, or leopards. A young panda often scampers up a tree if it's in danger.

Panda cubs have fun chasing each other in the trees.

A panda cub starts to walk when it is three or four months old.

Playtime

Young pandas love to play. They climb trees—and sometimes fall out of them if they haven't figured out how to climb down. They like tumbling and wrestling with their mother. Even older pandas will roll on the ground and do somersaults.

This young panda is enjoying playtime on his own.

Sometimes they also play and splash in the water. Playing helps to build up a panda's muscles.

Playing is even more fun with a friend!

Zoo pandas are often more playful than pandas in the wild, and keepers give them toys so they won't get bored. Zoo pandas play with plastic containers, cans, bags, or blocks of ice with food treats inside.

Leaving home

By the time it's a year old, a young panda can find all of its own food. But it stays with its mother until it is two or three years old. After that, many young pandas stay in territories near their mother, but some young female pandas travel far from home.

A panda is ready to start its own family when it is about five or six years old. Scientists believe that most wild pandas live about 20 years.

This young panda is almost as big as his mother. Soon he'll have to live on his own.

Most zoo pandas live longer than wild pandas. The oldest known zoo panda lived to be 34 years old. Researchers study zoo pandas to learn how to help wild pandas survive.

Grown-up pandas usually stay away from each other, but this mother and son seem very happy chewing bamboo together.

Panda fact file

Here is some more information about giant pandas. Your mom and dad might like to read this so you can talk about pandas some more when you see them at the zoo, or perhaps you can read these pages together.

Giant panda

The giant panda is a mammal. It belongs to the bear family, but people used to think that giant pandas belonged to the raccoon family. The lesser panda, also called the red panda, is part of the raccoon family and looks much more like a raccoon than a bear.

Where giant pandas live

Wild giant pandas live only in bamboo forests in the mountains of southwest China.

Panda numbers

Giant pandas are now very rare. Scientists think that there are only about 1,600 giant pandas living in the wild. Large areas of the forests where they live have been cut down, and many pandas were captured and killed by poachers in the past. Now, pandas and the areas where they live are very strictly protected, but some pandas are still killed by poachers.

Size

The giant panda is about four to five feet
(1.2–1.5 m) long, with a short tail of about
five inches (12 cm). It weighs 165 to 350 pounds
(75–160 kg). A newborn baby panda weighs
only 3.5 ounces (100 g), but by the time it's about
3 months old, it weighs up to 13 pounds (5.8 kg).

Find out more

If you want to learn more about pandas, check out
these Web sites:

World Wildlife Fund: Pandas
http://www.worldwildlife.org/pandas

Smithsonian National Zoological Park: Giant Pandas
http://www.nationalzoo.si.edu/Animals/giantpandas

San Diego Zoo: Giant Panda
http://www.sandiegozoo.org/animalbytes/t-giant_panda.html

ARKive Images of Life on Earth
http://www.arkive.org/species/GES/mammals/Ailuropoda_melanoleuca

Glossary

Cub
A young animal.

Dawn
First thing in the morning when the sun comes up.

Enclosure
The area where an animal lives in the zoo.

Gallop
A fast movement made by a four-legged animal.

Gland
A part of the body that makes a special substance, such as the liquid pandas use to leave scent messages.

Mammal

A warm-blooded animal, usually with four legs and at least some hair on its body. Female mammals feed their babies with milk from their own body.

Mate

To produce babies.

Nutrients

The things in food that keep a body healthy and help it grow.

Poacher

Someone who hunts an animal illegally.

Territory

The area where an animal spends most of its time and finds its food.

Index